D1194960

Shell

Shell

JUL 11 2008

Olive Senior

PROPERTY OF
SENECA COLLEGE
LIBRARIES
NEWNHAM CAMPUS

WITHDRAWN

A 4 A.M. BOOK

INSOMNIAC PRESS

Copyright © by Olive Senior 2007

All rights reserved. No part of this publication may be reproduced, stored in a retrieval system or transmitted, in any form or by any means, without the prior written permission of the publisher or, in the case of photocopying or other reprographic copying, a licence from Access Copyright, 1 Yonge Street, Suite 1900, Toronto, ON M5E 1E5

Library and Archives Canada Cataloguing in Publication

Senior, Olive
Shell / Olive Senior.

Poems.
ISBN 978-1-897178-48-5

I. Title.

PS8587.E552S54 2007   C811'.54   C2007-904518-9

The publisher gratefully acknowledges the support of the Canada Council, the Ontario Arts Council, and the Department of Canadian Heritage through the Book Publishing Industry Development Program.

Printed and bound in Canada

Insomniac Press
192 Spadina Avenue, Suite 403
Toronto, Ontario, Canada, M5T 2C2
www.insomniacpress.com

Text design and typesetting: Alysia Shewchuk

Canada Council Conseil des Arts
for the Arts du Canada

ONTARIO ARTS COUNCIL
CONSEIL DES ARTS DE L'ONTARIO

Canada

Also by Olive Senior

Poetry
Talking of Trees
Gardening in the Tropics
Over the Roofs of the World

Fiction
Summer Lightning
Arrival of the Snake-Woman
Discerner of Hearts

Non-fiction
The Message Is Change
A-Z of Jamaican Heritage
Working Miracles: Women's Lives in the English-
*   Speaking Caribbean*
Encyclopedia of Jamaican Heritage

Contents

GASTROPODA

You think I've stayed home all my life,
moving at snail's pace, sneakily living off
another's labour? You think I've nought
to leave behind but empty shell? Come:
study me. Take my chambered shell apart.
Brace yourself for whirlwinds
coiled at my heart.

Shell Out

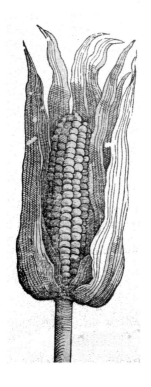

HATCH

what if
i didn't want out
if happy in here floating
from one end to the other
in this wachamacallit   one day
opened just a peepshow   crack
jump back girl   back from the
sound of breaking blast from the
light let in   once lines get crossed
there's no turning back flood waters
sweep me through the hatch   hello
world   tap   crumbling walls
shell   out   set me up
for life
for breaking

MAIZE

The first humans were created from corn.
— Popol Vuh: Las antiguas historias del Quiché

Mothers will understand this: The first ones I sent into the
world did alright, turned out to be human. But this lot!

Okay, perhaps I spoil them. Bearing them now, not solitary
and naked like the first but many together, gift-wrapped

in silky down and swaddling clothes of papery layer.
I've overdone it, perhaps, in the way of security and

comfort. For can I get them to leave? Even when
mature they continue to cling for dear life to me and –

worse – to each other. Unwrapped, without the light of day,
they know they are useless but are still so shy, they are

prepared to die – together. To live, they must be forcibly
undressed and separated. That's where my human children

come in. Skilled at brutality, they will happily rip these
children from me, strip off their clothing, pull them apart.

Because I know it's for their own good, I happily watch as
each little one pops out like a pearl. Ivory. Golden. Milky.

Not all will stay that way. Some will be dried, popped, parched, ground to be drunk or eaten. But I smile even as I

am myself cut down as spent and useless, for I know enough of my progeny will be saved to be planted and

nurtured. Become, in their turn, mothers proudly displaying their clinging children in their green array. The little ones

still attached to their mother, still clinging to one another; undercover, in the dark. Scared of the single life. Yet

dying for exposure. To grow up. To ripen the germ of Sun Father.

SHELTER

Growth rings inscribe
inside each shell
the markers of
a former life.

This shell, my skin,
outers a life
still stretched
still lived in.

GARDEN SNAIL

Snail locks up his mobile home for winter
pretends he's not at home
and goes to sleep.

For goodness' sake!
Who, when Spring comes
will tell him to awake? And how?

Who but the landlord of this trailer park
who dares to yell:
'Peel off and shell out. Now.'

TAÍNO GENESIS

We the people of Cacibajagua emerged
from the cave the moment Sun's longest leg
splintered the horizon. All went well except that
the sentry posted at the entrance at his first sight
of Sun blinked. Unwary sentinels cannot go
unpunished. With his eyes eclipsed who knows
what could have slipped through his grasp?
So Our Maker turned him into stone for his
tardiness and there he stands still: Macocael –
He-of-the-insomniac-eyes, our petrified eternal
guardian. We filed out expectantly, each one
trying not to cough and break the spell
as Sun's eye cracked open like guinep shell
and released us. We emerged dressed in our naked
best, not yet possessed of the feathers and beads
or the red anotto paint, the gift of Sun Father,
colour of worship and warrior, of
Hummingbird's iridescence. We would come
into the world stained black with our sacred
juice, guinep, colour of difficult passage
and tumescence. We would bleach in the sun
for nine days; then to the water to gather
the sacred herb digo, for the washing
to remove the last traces of our birth passage.
Guinep stain running like rain till
we reached again bare skin, our palette ready
for our first painting. Oh! Before
inscribing our names we should mention that

there was another cave, that of Amayauna –
the others, the people who do not matter
(to our story). We were Taíno, the ones gifted
with guinep or *jagua*. With sacred *bixa:* the herb
anotto. The ones shelled out by Sun Father.

CASSAVA/YUCA

When the Seven Sisters signal rain, the mothers make ready: cradle cassava sticks for planting, like children in their baskets.

To each they offer the incense of tobacco. Water with their tears. Buried under each grave mound: their people's future here.

> Radiate roots penetrate Mother Earth,
> douse for water. Children of Yuca
> shoot up high, fertilized by Sun Father.

In their gardens, the mothers softly tread, in dread lest they awaken sleeping child of Yuca without reason. Pray for the day the newly risen one cries out:

Cut me down. For you, I die each season. This is my body. Come, dig me, peel me, grate me, squeeze me, dry me, sift me, spread me, heat me.

Give me life again. Eat me.

SKIN

(After viewing Fernando Botero's work)

He's rumbled them, sketched them skin
stretched taut as drum.

Leaving flesh to make its ample statement
is so wise.

The rhythms of their stories freeze us
in black pearl eyes.

PEARL

Trophy wife, power object, your lustre fading
from neglect: Pull that rope from around your neck.

Don't you want to be free? Come now, break the spell.
Let each pearl be. Or cast them before swine. What

have you to lose? Honour, like the pearl, is already used.

Keep a single pearl for contemplation of the kingdom
within, or ingest it for melancholy, madness, and other

lunar folly. Better yet, count it a blessing, save for
longevity. Too many lives already lost for this string.

THE SKIN OF THE EARTH

(for Lyndal Osborne)

As startling in this gallery as pomander
of clove and orange, material from matter:
kelp, grass, stalk, stem, seed, and pith. All
return alive in the hands of the artist.
The essence not what we consume but what
remains and speaks to us across the room,
contained by its own weight as gesture, as
skeletal mountains of stalk, of skin.

So too we could lie, mountains of bones
beneath the skin of Earth that quietly
fashions our return. Not in that self-same
shell, that edifice of body, but encoded
in found matter like perfume
strong as clove, bittersweet as orange.
Tantalizing essence of what was once
the ripeness of ourselves.

SAILOR'S VALENTINE

Long after he is gone, a message
from a further shore arrives, the token
of a love alive. The wooden box
that sailors make for sweethearts
to display the lovingly collected
tribute shells in disingenuous array:

Helmets, false tritons, limpets, abalones,
whelks, olives, mitres, marginellas,
nutmeg and heart cockles....

On top, the message spells
in purple murex shells: 'Remember me.'

She gazes into the open box and feels imperilled, feels
the undertow of old wounds gaping, feels
the wavering before her eyes
       till she summons up the tearing that will cauterize,
that will flood the shells and speed them back her valentine,
draining back to the grave, the empty sea.

C A N O E
O C E A N

permit me to skim your surface only my line
a little scratch my net a tickle my catch
like mites reaped from some great beast's hide

down deeper? o no thank you the drowned
gnaw songs of hunger in that kingdom underwater
swallow splinters of gnashed pride wondering
how did they transgress?

i will just humbly take a little fish here
and try not to upset

HURRICANES

Winds that are born out of thin air beyond the Gulf
bring other heartaches than hurricanes.

Hurricanes expose these empty shelves in our lives.

Did you know they were there before the winds
signalled us?

LUCEA HARBOUR

Importunate waves run ceaselessly to kiss the shore.
O rigid land, so indifferently receiving them.

THE SONG THAT IT SINGS

        so far from the sea I find myself
worldless. (Oh, leave it alone, but I meant
to write 'wordless.') And sometimes, like

tonight, I feel a hemispheric sadness: the
New World as tired as the rest. And there's
a waterlogged moon getting ready to burst

like the gourd that spilled an ocean when
the seeker, like myself, disobeyed, took it
down from where it hung by a thread,

dropped and broke it. So how were we
to know that from it seas would stream
forth, bringing three ships with our eclipse:

the Black Sun? Yet how but by disobedience
can we change the world order? So what if
all we are left with is a sieve to carry water?

We can use it to fish up a poem or two
to sail from our flagpoles. Or plant vines
to swim seeking radiate air, colonizing

the light to store it for rebirth: a summer
virgin in lace-mantle
of silver.

So excuse me for interjecting an ode here
to silver: to my vine of such magical growth,
and to moonlight, to starlight, to fish-scales,

to sighs, to sadness and whispers, to the pure light,
to water, to ripples over stone, to veils, to jewels
and cutlery, to tinsel, to glitter, to winners' cups

and chalices, to the lining of clouds, to watch cases,
to the instruments before steel, to erasures,
to anniversaries, to the snail's trail, to mother-

of-pearl, to musical notes that are liquid. To our
Earth seen from space, to the light of the fireflies,
to ice, to crystal – petrification of light,

to reflections of mirrors – the soul's shining.
To luminescence of eels, dust particles,
electricity. To anguish and the colour

of forgetting. To needles and pinpricks,
to the pure heart, the clear conscience,
the firm voice. To the keening that is never ending.

For the ocean is endless, the sea has no corners,
no turnings, no doors. And none can silence this song
that it sings.

Shell Blow

SHELL BLOW

I

Flesh is sweet but disposable, what counts
is shell. Like other objects beached, beyond
your ken, inert I lie, bleached and toneless

save for ocean song that only visitors claim
to hear. What if one day you accidentally
picked up the right shell – such as I; placed it

to your ear, pressed – by chance – the right
knob, there would pour out not the croak
of song soaked up in sea-water and salt

but the real thing, a blast-out, everybody's
history: *areito, canto histórico,* a full
genealogy of this beach, this island people.

You could be blown away by what is held
custody here, every whorl a book of life,
a text, a motion picture, a recording,

or what passes for such in our island
version. You could begin anywhere.
Encoded in are full facilities for fast forward,

play, playback and dub, reversible though
not scrubbable. For we – as you know –
are master engineers when it comes to

scratching out a living on vinyl, on dutty
or plantation. We is Ginnal at the Controls!
Nansi Nation. We can rib it up, dibble it,

rub it, dub it and fracture it. Splice it. Spice
it up. But like a spite, we still can't find
a way to erase not one word. They say,

that is how History stay. Say you bound
to re-live it on and on. Unless you can find
a way to shell it out; pass it on.

PASS IT ON!

II

May we speak as I once did in tandem
with the old trumpet player, Shell-man
of the village who positioning me to his lips,

too-tooted out the notes to mark our
Angelus of work every day of the year?
Shell-blow for our mournings, our birthings,

to recount genealogies. For alarms
and warnings, for summons to meetings,
for connecting with the next hill.

Shell-man our bell-ringer, shell our telephone
to heaven and elsewhere. But I noticed
it got harder and harder for Shell-man

to blow notes that worth anything. People
no longer hearing, not wanting to listen
over the noise coming in. Harder for me

to give out when I couldn't take in
what was happening in our world. Heart
so full, nothing resounding. The emptiness

tunnelling the brains of the children,
noise of the cities trawling them in. Shell-man
lost and faded, castaway and toneless as shell.

III

O what tidings I could pour into the right ear,
perhaps yours? The real thing, what the
ordinary visitor would not hear. Every time

shell blow, we exhale another tale. Shall we
give it a whirl? So go on. What you waiting for?
Pick me up. Let us sit mouth to ear. Let me

put my tongue in, just for practice. There.
Are you scared? Do you find that thrilling?
Disturbing? Tintillating? Or simply wet?

Would you prefer to hear ocean roar? O
I can offer so much more than that old
croak soaked up in salt water, burning sand.

I want to woo you. Till you rue the day
you listened, for there's no turning back
till we get to the bottom of the rhythm:

too-toot of the conch, the funk of shak-shak.
By next shell-blow you blue and black.
For is head to head we have to go or if you

prefer toe to toe, wherever you have feeling
I am willing to go reeling off my song. For
it's too long I've been lying here forsaken –

since ol'time someting done weh – and I been
trying to reconnect to the centre of that whorl.
To have someone press that button, to say

HEY, MAN! LISSEN! IT'S THE DAMNDEST
THING! COME: PUT THIS SHELL TO YOUR
EAR. AS SURE AS HELL THERE'S

SOMETHING GOING ON IN HERE!

Say what?

PASS IT ON!

IV

Baby, I want you. I want to be your creature
of legend called Dry-head, the one once you
take it up you can never put it down. Unless

you find a way to pass it on. Like Burr-Lady,
Clinging-Woman, like the Rolling Head, Dry
Skull, that still be walking, talking, looking for

a way to reconnect with some living-breathing
body, and go hoist itself on top of you.
If your hand just pass over the button or you

eye-pass the page – just a glance or glancing
blow – know you taking up trouble, you
hoisting history on your back that I been trying

to download, to unload the years. So full
I stuff there's no space for the new.
Once shell stop blow is like time

stand still for people. As if they come into
the world just so. Been marking time
ever since. Convinced their name is Nobody,

born in a place that is called Nothing, for
it is Historyless. For History is invention
and nothing invent yaso according to

Famous Author that was the last
I was to hear about before all over
the Caribbean shell by any name stop blow:

kaachi, lambie, panchajanya, futoto.
And isn't it surreal that I'm stuffed so full
of history yet the only reel in my head is

that 'nothing/nothing' mantra that is like
that stone that got thrown down into
the Caribbean basin, rippling out to form

the arc of islands (so said other Famous
Author) then sinking, sinking into itself,
into *nada?*

For one who's been around as long as me
it's hard to bear; that's why I'm begging you
to lend me your ear. I will thank you,

praise song you. But beware! Once I grab you,
you can't do a thing, can never fling me off,
for the more you throw, the tighter I cling.

Better to relax. Listen and learn. No harm
ever come of that. Say: Yes, free paper burn.
Back to school again. Shell it out. Pop 'tory gimme.

First Lesson:
Faut al'la pou con la
'You must go there to know there.'

PASS IT ON!

SEND THE FOOL A LITTLE FURTHER

Likl bwoy, come here. Is April Fool Day. Tek this message to that lady you see there. Do as she say. Make sure you don't tek fas' open it up so read – I will know; I will give you bus' ass! Plus you would find out it say: Send the fool a little further. Heh-heh.

Shell Shock

'The story of a lump of sugar is a whole lesson in
political economy, in politics, and also in morality.'
— Auguste Cochin, quoted in Manuel Moreno
Fraginals' *Sugar Mill*

QUASHIE'S SONG

Here the John Crows wheel
And the whip keeps time
And the days dip by
And the sun keeps turning
And the seasons fly
And I'm old, old, in a flash.

When was I ever young?

PEPPERCORN

Torn from the vine in a place of moist
heat and shade where I was growing,
skin once plump and reddish, glowing.
Suddenly, a job lot. Indiscriminately
thrown in, we are jumbled, shaken up,
rolled together, little knowing our fate
or destination, till black and shrivelled
by the sun, looking all alike now, we are
tumbled into hold of a ship for forty days
and forty nights (we guess – for black
is the fenestration).

Disgorged, spilled out, shell-shocked
I come parched and dried, my head
emptied, till shock-still I come to rest,
shelled out, buck naked. In the mad
ensuing scramble, who will come
            who will come sample me,
view me, choose me, sort me out
for grade and quality, drive me home
to crush me, use me? Know that alone
I'm of little value, like a peppercorn
rental. All together, we can pepper
your arse with shot.

Over time, despite our treatment,
you'll see, survivors stay pungent
and hot. You can beat me senseless,
grind me down, crush me to bits, to
powder. You can never lose my bite
on your tongue, my hold on your senses:
forever I'll linger and cling.

In your mad scramble to possess,
devour me, remember, if you'd only
allow me to do a striptease, slow, peel off
my black skin, you'd be pleased –
or shocked – to discover: I'm white below.

SWEET
BWOY

Let's get just one thing
straight, right? Beneath this
fine, upstanding pose, this self-
contained exterior, I'm absolutely,
totally, in control. Sure, I'll let you
extract from me whatever you
desire – if you can pay the price.
So go ahead: grind me, juice me,
reduce me, fire me up, refine me,
till I yield what you want: this
shattered white crystal. Or – if
you like dark meat – this sticky
brown bag variety. I'm malleable.
I can crawl crude and slow like
molasses. I can also get spiritual,
transparent as rain, take you higher
with a kick that is deadly – I am
purest with age. Then I can
sweeten you, calm your rage.

I can't hide my origins; under-
neath, I'm raw and I'm crude,
I've a terrible reputation. Yea, I'm
brutal, a user of men, consumer of
acreage, the more virgin the better.
I love it when the forests burn to
prep the ground for me. When – just

to serve – millions are captured and
shipped across the sea. Okay, those
good old days are gone but slave
consumers – like you – are still born
every second. That's why I'm in the
driver's seat. I dictate the rhythm.
My seasons not spring, summer,
winter, but strictly rotated by
my needs: planting, reaping,
croptime. Then what they call
ha-ha! – the dead season.

For a brief spell, I give you
room. Recovering from excess,
I put down roots, send up shoots.
Each year, like a sickness I bloom.
For I'm the only one allowed to
flower. Fire my signature. I burn
human fuel. I dictate the rhythm
of the dance. I grow as tall as I
please, then do a slow striptease,
as armies move to chop me down.
But life is a battleground and I'll
always rise again. My recovery
quick, I come armed with the
weapons for battle: my razor-
sharp edges, my fuzz to work its
way under your skin. I choke
you with my lingering smell,
cover everywhere with my litter.

I can seduce young and old
with my upstanding demeanour,
pixilate them with my juice. Yes,
I'm the outsider, the interloper.
I've crossed the world to serve
you. I give you harvest: full belly.
An illusion. I sap the soil, end
fertility. I'll drive you to penury,
abandon you, move on. Yes, I'm
wild and I'm wicked. I'm arrogant.
I don't care. You'll find me every-
where. I don't discriminate. I'm
your foremost addiction. Your
kind will always treat me well. I
guarantee satisfaction.

CANE GANG

Torn from the vine from another world
to tame the wildness of the juice, assigned
with bill and hoe to field or factory, chained
by the voracious hunger of the sugar cane

the world's rapacious appetite for sweetness

How place names of my servitude mock me:
Eden, Golden Vale, Friendship, Green Valley,
Hermitage, Lethe, Retreat, Retirement, Content,
Paradise, Pheonix, Hope, Prospect, Providence

Each with the Great House squatting
on the highest eminence
the Sugar Works overlooking
my master's eye unyielding
the overseer unblinking
not seeing
the black specks
                floating across
                        their finely crafted
                                landscape

At shell blow assembled the broken-down
bodies, the job-lots scrambled into gangs

like beads on a string O not pearls no just
unmatched pairings the random bindings
like cane trash no not like the cane pieces
laid out geometric and given names
and burning.

WEST INDIA CANE PIECE RAT (1821)

What is lower than a rat?
I'm lower than that.

For Rat can climb, can wriggle and work its way out
of the trap. Rat can flap and jump to freedom.

What's better than that?

I sink to my knees in mud, rain or shine, weeding
the canefields, hoeing the line. Rat doesn't plant
but it reaps what's mine, or rather what's Massa's, for I
don't own a thing. While Rat is free, Massa owns me.

I'm lower than a rat.

Rat breeds as it likes, rat pikni never done.
Slave woman work like mule, we can't breed none.
And if we drop in our trace like Massa other beast,
he don't give a damn, plenty more where we come from.

What is worse than that?

The only thing I'm sure of as I hoe Massa cane
is that when Rat die, him not coming back again.
Not a soul going cry as Ratta turn back into dirt, as him
burn with the cane-trash, as him vanish from the earth.

Seh who better than Rat?
I better than that.

For I know that if I'm careful and I eat no salt.
If I don't mek Massa limb me, if I hold on to mi head
If I sing King Zambi song while I live in this here prison,
the minute that I'm dead, I fly straight back to Guinea.

What a day of rejoicing on that other shore, when the
nine nights are over and I'm home once more.
With the dead, with the living, with the children yet-to-be
in the bosom of my family I will once again be free.

So what you say now, Mister Rat?
What is better than that!

CANEFIELD SURPRISED BY EMPTINESS

It is not so much the shell shock as questions
we never asked that leave us cowering still
among the dead sugar metaphors.

Is this a legacy or something for which I am still
expected to pay? The circle on dust left by ghost
mules turning widdershins, turning the ghost
mills, turning the cane stalks into questions:

Are cane-cutters' children destined to rise,
like stalks, bloom like cane tassels, or to sink,
rootwise, into anger ratooning still?

Still as the closed circle of the mill.
Still as the knife blade descending.

This still life could wear us down.

WALKING ON EGGS

hanging
        onto

knowing
        not knowing

the contours of the minefield
        the trigger point
the charge

        knowing
not knowing

the reversals possible
        between madness
and cupidity
        extraction
and loaded gun
        between croptime
and planting
        fertility
and empty shell

I feel sometimes collected
        sometimes breakable

&
mindful

always
mind full of you.

WHAT COULD BE WRITTEN ON A GRAIN OF RICE

Far from *Kun-Lun*
the crane's legs tied

I swallow the unfamiliar
with each breath.

Ku-li – bitter strength –
bound to sugar cane fields

to a circular season.
When my servitude ends

to mud I'll indenture.
Plant familiar green

seedlings yielding grain
hard as tropic.

Bitter strength
husking promise.

Futures written
on this grain:

the sight of
Kun-Lun.

FISHING IN THE WATERS WHERE MY DREAMS LIE

I

The day my master sent me fishing for his
          dinner
is the best day up to now I can remember.

This sea I found was not the sea that bound
          and swallowed me
that brought me hither, delivered me as less
          than what I left behind.
Here no looming seaside barracoons nor
          tattered sails nor the waves'
blue keening. What opened my eyes were
          the colours the sun
broke up on the water. Alone in my dugout
          shell, I dropped
my line and waited with baited breath,
          explored a vacancy
on my tongue. For here in this new world it is
          my master
who gives things names and here I am struck
          dumb, not knowing
how to summon them from the deep, what song
          to sing them
          so they'll leap.

O keepers of the deep release the catch or let
my master's vengeance fill this empty net.

By the powers of
Yemoja-Oboto
Agbe-Naete
Aizan-Velekete
Avrekete
Gede
Agoué
Olókun

II

I'm homing these waters
now I sing the joys of knowing
scales fall from my eyes hail
my brothers that swim from my
homeland to greet me here
clothed in the same bright dress
wearing new names

Each night I dream my net breaks up water
as water breaks up the shell-like image of the moon.

Praises I sing now to:

Agwé
Madre de Agua
Yemayá
Olókun

AT THE SLAVE MUSEUM

The slave ship shell-shock dark
as the night-filled gourd

Cavernous as a grave fault

The viewer's mind
stretches to fit.
Fails to grasp

          until

we come to it

the child's body flexed
not yet shelled out.

At the heart of this search
something breaks

Outside: The Sun has his eye on

the truth that spirals out of ( )hell.

PICTURE

We who fear exposure most are cursed
with eyes demanding wholeness. Not
what the painter sees: the charming,
lying version, the picturesque. O no.
Not like that here. This retina assembles
fractured images only, repairs the shattered
pieces. Trawls for evidence in shadowed
light, traces fleeting fragments in ghostly
black and white. The impetus: to close
the circle, to seek transparency, to open
the shutter wide
                to hold it steady. Receive
the measured quantity of light.

Snap!

               this incarnate, wholesome, image.

Shelter

FOUND POEM REGARDING ARCHEOLOGICAL CONCERNS

Broken and fragmented material
recovered through excavation

quantifiable

patterns observable in the frequency and
distribution of discarded

goods

JOIN-THE-DOTS

*In the sample of 282 plantation maps drawn from the
National Library of Jamaica's collection, some 25 per cent
show the "village" area as a blank.*
— Barry Higman, *Jamaica Surveyed*

We played at Join-the-Dots, Grandma and me,
but never could we win the prize.
For I saw pictures she could not see.
They said I had clear-seeing eyes.

Our house was built on land where once
a village stood. Where fragments
floating in the air sometimes cried out
for personhood.

They pounded on the rooftop, tore at
the gutter. 'Hush, it is the wind,'
Grandma said, but I knew better
though I would never

utter a word. For I was sworn to secrets.
'This is where we once lived too,'
the children said. 'We'd like
to play with you.'

When I could not sleep for black dots
floating, Grandma said, 'Hush,
I'll bring you cocoa-tea sweetened
with cane sugar and

a hint of nutmeg. That will calm you
down.' I'd try to share it with my
ghostly friends who said they
lived in land-snail shells

and sailed all night the village round.
Their Old One said: 'No. You drink up,
child. For this our bodies
turned to dust. Ground

into fields of sugar cane, of cocoa-walks,
of nutmeg groves. Drink.
In remembrance of us.'
I'd drain the cup.

The cocoa, cane sugar, the nutmeg, touched me
so sweetly, I'd sleep long. Sleep deeply.

SHELL

From the Great House shell, we salvage bricks,
we pick up sticks, we never throw away.
We use things up as we are used. What can we
leave to speak of us?
      We do not eat off sets of plate or dine
in state or even sit at table. Our fragile artefacts
a yabba, monkey jar, our calabashes, mortar,
a cast-iron pot (from massa's store), a grinding
stone. These alone with our firestick, our
kreng-kreng basket, our three smooth firestones
form our domestic hearth, our altar.

So if in years to come some people
might be mad enough to search for us,
to trace our passing, they would have
to dig deep to find us here, sift ashes,
measure bones and beads and shell discarded.
      Just as the men long ago
digging the foundations of the Great House
my grandfather did say, came across fragments
of the true landowners, the ones before us,
the ones whose bones they buried under fill.
The 'Indian' people that once possessed it,

and possess us still.

THE FIRST HOUSE

Homeless, Deminán and his brothers,
orphaned and wandering forefathers,
Winds of Four Quarters, blew hither
and yon until

Turtle-Woman stopped them
in their tracks: the first mating. Said:
I am ready for nesting. Said: Build me
a house. Untrained but undaunted
(in the way of such heroes) they each
took a corner of the world, stood like
pillars to anchor it, and strained and
puffed to lift high the roof of sky,
which billowed out and in (they had
a hell of a time controlling it) until
it righted itself and domed into
the model of Turtle-Woman's shell.

And so we were born in the House
of our Great Mother, our crabbed
and comforting genitor, who still bears
our first house on her back.

S(H)IFT

I

dig

here

sift and measure and
keep on miss
           ing me

                      there
on pathways
unrecorded
ephemeral
as snail trail
ing silver un
der fences by
passing bound
aries evad
ing cartography

here

       picture me
       as background fill
       black dots inch
       ing stead
       ily for
       ward
       to fill –

ah
you blinked

missed

       the pathways of the lash
       inscribed on my back
       the calligraphy of burning
       on my fettered wrists

missed
the place where I house a knot
where memory thickens and pearls.

II

Sift

our fragile fetishes of power:
eggshell, feather, powdered horn,
grave dirt and endurance.
                    Shift –

Yes
I invested in dress, in adornment.
A life too short for the weight of
accumulation
            for provision
beyond
this
very sunset

When I'll be

born again
born again

my soul hidden
in shell

spiralling
down to clear water
to the valleys of the sea
where the turquoise bleeds into indigo
entrapping eternity.

Empty Shell

William Beckford Jr., called by Lord Byron 'England's richest son,' never once saw the source of his wealth.

In March 1787 he boarded a ship in England to visit his Jamaican plantations but got off at the first stop, Lisbon. He wrote in a letter: 'The more I hear of Jamaica, the more I dread the climate, which I fully expect will wither my health away....you must excuse my going any further....'

When Beckford died (at Bath in 1844) The Times described him as 'One of the very few possessors of great wealth who have honestly tried to spend it poetically.'

A SUPERFICIAL READING

*(An eighteenth-century painting of the titled English lady
and her black child slave)*

Turn the page and revel in the surface opulence
of moiré silk, of creamware, pearlware, skin.
The shell-like ear behind the torque of ringlets,

the black pearl eyes. The pose is classical.
She does not really notice you within the triangle
of her body and embracing arm not sheltering,

more like cold marble. You kneel and the painter
collapses your upper body into a sign:
a small black triangle. Her touch is light, for you

are a page she cannot read or write on. You are
an accessory to fashion, like the pearl choker
loaned you for the occasion which collars you

and separates your head from your body
(reminding you of an earlier truncation). There is
no mind over matter, for you are owned. You

exist merely to make her seem more luminous.
She does not know that perfection is shadowed
always, like a phantom limb. She does not know

about inversion and that the right hand never
shows what the left is doing. So that your prop,
that fake offering of shell like Pandora's box

could spill and pearl her skin like a sickness,
bloom like stigmata with no Erzulie here
to plead for her, no Santiago de Compostela

to intercede. She does not know you are
the Sable Venus-in-waiting, the black pearl
poised to be borne on cusp of emptied shell.

THE POETICS OF A WEST INDIA DINNER PARTY

(mid-seventeenth century) *

First then (because beefe being the greatest rarity in the
Island, especially such as this is) I will begin with it,
and of that sort there are these dishes at either messe,
a Rumpe boyl'd,
a Chine roasted,
a large piece of the brest roasted, the Cheeks bak'd, of
        which is a dish to either messe,
the tongue and part of the tripes minc'd for Pyes, season'd
        with sweet Herbs finely minc'd, suet, Spice, and
        currans;
the legges, pallets and other ingredients for an Olio Podrido
to either messe, a dish of Marrow-bones,
so here are 14 dishes at the Table and all of beefe;
and this he intends as the great Regalio, to which he
invites
        his fellow planters; who having well eaten of it,
        the dishes are taken away,

and another Course brought in, which is
a Potato pudding,
a dish of Scots collips of a legge of Porke, as good
        as any in the world,
a fricasy of the same,
a dish of boyl'd Chickens,
a shoulder of younge Goate drest with his blood and tyme,
a Kid with a pudding in his belly,
a sucking Pig, which is there the fattest whitest and

sweetest in the world, with the fragrant sauce of
the brains, salt, sage and Nutmeg done with
Claret wine,

a shoulder of Mutton which is there a rare dish,

a Pasty of the side of a young Goate, and a side of a fat
young Shot upon it, well season'd with Pepper
and salt, and with some Nutmeg,

a loyne of Veale, to which there wants no sauce being so
well finisht with Oranges, Lymons, and Lymes,

three young Turkies in a dish,

two Capons, of which sort I have seen some extreme large
and very fat,

two henns with eggs in a dish,

four Ducklings, eight Turtle Doves and three Rabbets;
and for cold bak'd meats,

two Muskovie Ducks larded, and seasoned well with
pepper and salt;

and these being taken off the Table,

another course is set on, and that is

of Westphalia or Spanish bacon,

dried Neats Tongues,

Botargo,

pickled Oysters,

Caviare,

Anchovies,

Olives and (intermixt with these) Custards, Creams, some
alone, some with preserves of Plantines, Banana,
Guavers, put in, and those preserv'd alone by
themselves,

Cheese-cakes,

Puffes, which are to be made with English flower, and
        bread, for the Cassavie will not serve for this
        kind of cookerie;
sometimes Tansies, sometimes Froizes or Amulets, and for
        fruite, Plantines, Bananoes, Guavers, Milions,
        prickled Peare, Anchove Peare, Prickled Apple,
        Custard Apple, water Milions, and Pines worth
        all that went before.
To this meat you seldom faile of this drink, Mobbie,
        Beveridge, Brandy, Kill-Divell, Drink of the
        Plantine, Claret wine, White wine, and Renish
        wine, Sherry, Canary, Red sack, wine of the Fiall,
        with all spirits that come from England.

*Taken word for word (and arranged 'poetically')
from Richard Ligon,* A True & Exact History of the
Island of Barbados *(London, 1657)*

AUCTION

I

The poetics of men who rose from nothing but auctions
from slave-ships, from piracy and smuggling, who pulled

themselves up by the canestalk, ratooned rich as eastern
potentates, retiring to England to don the furs and golden

chains of office, to embed themselves at the heart of its
civic institutions, its rotten boroughs, the only place to feel

at home in. Buying their way into society, ennobling
their progeny. Nesting like exotic species around London's

Georgian squares. Till, sickened by memory, haunted
by the smell of burning canefields, of boiling sugar,

molasses, rum, bagasse, of blackened sweated labour,
dying of ostentation, they retire, ill and overfed, to Bath,

'to sucke in some of the sweet ayre of England,' to expire,
leaving behind a spurious genealogy. Erased the ignoble

birth, the slackness, any hint of blackness, save on the page,
the black boy as accessory with silver dog collar, dressed

and possessed as adornment to highlight wealth, to
heighten whiteness. To iconize imperial distance.

II

And at the 'plundering frontiers of Empire,'
the powerful father, who built his own oriental
palace, his Egyptian Hall, who sired English

bastards, on whose death Chatterton wrote
an ode, who hired the nine-year-old Mozart
to teach his infant son musical composition,

rich and powerful enough to publicly call
the English nobility subalterns to the body of
the nation. And yet to his Lord Mayor's banquet

they come, 600 dishes served on gold plate.
In attendance: 6 Dukes, 2 Marquises, 23 Earls,
4 Viscounts, 14 Barons and 18 Baronets.

His legitimate heir destined to become
England's richest son. Yet after all that gilded
promise, so despised, so alone, so shunned.

O what can fill this emptiness?

III

Taste and beauty over-cultivated.
The planter planting the Rose Garden,
Thornery, Pinetum, the Alpine Garden –
epitome of the sublime, the picturesque.

At auction, books and paintings bought and sold
in lots
        like slaves
                fondled

as my master in far-off England
                              fondles
the rare book he purchases, examines
for age and shape, hefts for weight,
caresses for surface scratches, tests
the latches
        the hide toughened
like the leather bindings
my master unties
                cuts
the bound sheets to view the inside and finds
the white pages covered O
covered with such tiny black fragments.

O my word!

My master takes home the latest acquisition
for his collection, borne by six footmen in
gold and embroidery. Alone, the man on whom

no neighbours would call enters his barbaric
high tower furnished in gold, crimson, scarlet,
purple and ebony. Alone, he sits to decipher
the black markings, his feet propped upon
an antique footstool: a kneeling blackamoor.

To find
        each letter, ant-like, running together
in a black connecting trail. A coffle. A sentence.

My master reads in silence. Alone. A cypher in a
hollow nest.

O what can fill this emptiness?

IV

What but the poetics of possessions, enough
to make the visitor 'dazzled and drunk with beauty'

    Greek vases of chalcedonian onyx
    Sevres china
    Egyptian porphyry
    Cabinet by Bernini
    Madame de Pompadour's black lacquer box
    Buhl armoires from the Louvre palace
    Ormolu chandeliers
    Mosaic tables of Florentine marble
    Persian carpets
    and
    Portrait of de Vos of Grotius
    Portrait of Rembrandt painted by himself
    Portrait of Pope Gregory, by Passerotti
    Portrait of Cosmo de Medici by Bronzino Allori
           ('fresh as if painted yesterday')
    and
    rusty helmets
    tattered shields
    inscriptions and broken milestones
    medals
    tessellated pavements
    shiploads of mutilated figures
    holy fragments
    pagan images
    and
    'purchases made in the teeth of the Holy Roman

Emporer and the King of France'
at the Duc de la Valiere's sale of the
century.

V

Not here
not here to disfigure the aesthetics, to mar
the poetics of Fonthill Tower, but locked in
the office of his London agent, his sugar factor,
the artefacts of high finance: beautifully engraved
Bills of Exchange.

Not here
the tedium of the counting house, the utter
boredom of grinding out so much money.

Not here
not here to sully the perfection
of the picturesque but under a vertical sun and
the eye of the nigger-driver,
hopping to it on his Jamaican plantations,
to turn the wheels that spin the green-cane into
gold-
      en sugar crystals
          tripping
                to a different poetic meter

          to prime the
      pumps
of a new technology,
    the industrial
      revolution
         in far-off England:

600 beautifully
scarred and
artistically
mutilated
black slaves.

VI

Here
no black page but a Swiss dwarf
and hundreds of volumes in choice old Morocco
bindings.

VII

To house it all the neo-Gothic Tower at Fonthill
aimed at eliciting sentiments of amazement,
shock and awe built in record time by my
master whom they called a 'nigger-driver' not
referring to his progenitor but for the way he
drove architects builders contractors gardeners
to complete in speed the 'Grand Babel' the
enchanted gardens and monastic demesne
locked within a wall twelve feet high and seven
miles long and gated,
                encircling 500 acres of a
'contrived, flowering wilderness' and Gothic
sham ruins.

If he had waited, in no time at all the ruin would
have become all too real. When the tower came
crashing down, he had already sealed a deal and
sold it.

VIII

How time and distance swallow the vanished
ruins, the mock glens and pastures, wild copse
and groves of pine. How the Wiltshire Downs
reclaim the artificiality of the picturesque.

Nothing remaining of vanished pride and tower
except the possessions auctioned, collected in
other citadels of power: libraries, museums,
galleries, castles, to gather dust in other empty

rooms where consumers still consume in
loneliness. Day after day, in gilded halls, the
servant armies vacuum, and wonder: Whence
comes this dust?
                O could it have been when
you introduced into your aristocratic domains,
for style and decorative effect, those black
pages?

Our fragile fetishes of power, our powdered
fragments, rise now to lightly dust these precious
artefacts, these hollowed shelves. And nothing
can stave off the relentless grinding down by

this new slavery: the collections, the recordings,
the writing of history. And none can shackle
passing time that is excavating from within, the
promise of the silenced voices: the resonance of
emptied shell.

Author's Note

These are poems sprouting from the sugar cane fields on islands drenched in blood, the former British West Indies.

I started writing the poems in this book many years earlier, but I wanted to be done with them by 2007, the 200th anniversary of the abolition of the slave trade by Britain.

The huge labour force required by the sugar cane plantations was the driving force behind the slave trade by which millions of Africans were captured and brought in chains to forced labour across the sea.

At one time, sugar made these small West Indian islands the most profitable to their European owners; wars were fought over them. At the close of the Seven Years War (1763), the tiny islands of Guadeloupe and Martinique were returned to the French in exchange for the undeveloped territory of Canada.

The sugar cane plant itself is a hard shell imprisoning the gold within. But that shell has to be beaten and crushed to release its sweet juice, the first step in making sugar, a chilling metaphor for the way millions of human beings were beaten and crushed in order to produce it.

Not much cane sugar is produced in the islands today, but the legacies of sugar are everywhere. For the plantation system was used as an instrument to malform societies, denude lands, traffic in people – all to create enormous wealth that flowed back overseas, to the 'Mother Country.'

The impetus for the shell motif in this book was a visit I made to Wiltshire, England, seeking the site of Fonthill Abbey, built at the height of plantation slavery as the grandest private house in Europe. Built by the man called 'England's richest son,' William Beckford Jr., whose wealth came from his family's Jamaican sugar plantations.

I didn't feel saddened that I could not find a single stone standing, because the story is no longer about that emptiness, the enterprise in ostentatious wealth and vanity. The story is now about us, the inheritors – on both sides of the Atlantic – and that emptied space waiting for the choices we make.

Shell Blow. Ready, steady, go!

Acknowledgements

I am grateful to the publishers of the following publications in which earlier versions of these poems first appeared:

The Literary Review of Canada, Sentinel Poetry (Online), The International Literary Journal, Journal of Postcolonial Writing, Kunapipi, Mangrove, Wasafiri, Poetry Wales, Calabash, Journal of West Indian Literature, Moving Worlds.

The following books were helpful in providing background information: Douglas V. Armstrong, *The Old Village and the Great House: An Archaeological and Historical Examination of Drax Hall Plantation, St. Ann's Bay, Jamaica*, Urbana: University of Illinois Press, 1990 (from which the 'Found Poem Regarding Archeological Concerns' p.67 is extracted). Peter Fryer, *Staying Power: The History of Black People in Britain*, London: Pluto Press, 1984. Derrick Knight, *Gentlemen of Fortune: The Men Who Made Their Fortunes in Britain's Slave Colonies*, London: Frederick Miller, 1978. James Lees-Milne, *William Beckford*, Tisbury, England: Compton Russell, 1976. Boyd Alexander, *England's Wealthiest Son: A Study of William Beckford*, London: Centaur Press, 1962. H. A. N. Brockman, *The Caliph of Fonthill*, London: Werner Laurie, 1956. John Rutter, *An Illustrated History and Description of Fonthill Abbey*, 1823.

As ever, I am grateful to my discerning editor, Paul Vermeersh, and to Mike O'Connor and the team at Insomniac Press. Thanks to Alysia Shewchuk, Dan Varrette, Gillian Rodgerson, and Gillian Urbankiewicz for helping to make it happen. And a special thank you to Andreas Oberli and Wenty Bowen for their pictures.

Picture Credits

P. 31 Wentworth Bowen for the photograph of 'The Unknown Maroon,' public monument, Republic of Haiti, by Albert Mangonès; p.65 photo by Andreas Oberli; p.78 National Portrait Gallery, London.

All other images are in the public domain.

Notes on Poems

The poems 'Taíno Genesis' (p. 18) and 'The First House' (p. 71) are retellings of the myths of the aboriginal Taíno of the Caribbean; first collected in *La Relación acerca de las Antigüedades de los Indios* by Fray Ramón Pané, c. 1498; new edition with notes by José Juan Arrom, Havana: Editorial Ciencias Sociales, 1990. 'Cassava/Yuca' (p. 20) is also based on Taíno beliefs and practices; the Seven Sisters refer to the Pleiades, the visible portion of the star cluster used to regulate planting; 'grave mound' refers to the fact that cassava or yuca was planted in huge mounds. Also Taíno is the myth of the sea coming from a broken gourd in 'The Song That It Sings' (p. 28).

'What Could Be Written on a Grain of Rice' (p. 58) references the indentured Chinese who, along with workers from India, were brought to work in the Caribbean sugar cane fields after the African slaves were freed: *Kun-lun* is the Daoist earthly paradise.

'Cane piece' in 'Cane Gang' (p. 51) refers to the sugar cane fields into which each plantation was divided.